D1118888

IF BOOKS

If You PLANT A SEED... AND OTHER NATURE PREDICTIONS

BY BLAKE A. HOENA

CAPSTONE PRESS
a capstone imprint

Open up your backdoor. Birds wing by and crickets chirp. Trees touch the sky and flowers bloom. Watch closely and you can predict the wonders that will happen. Want to give it a try?

The weather changes with each season. Summer is hot and sunny. Fall is cool and clammy. Winter can be cold and snowy, but what of spring? What's the weather like between frosty winter and sunny summer?

ANSWER

Spring is cool because the weather is changing from a cold season, winter, to a hot one, summer. Spring is also rainy. It's the time of year when plants begin to grow.

It's a cold wintery day. Snow covers the ground, but your friends want to go outside and play. How will they dress for the cold weather?

ANSWER

Mittens and boots, sweaters and scarves, and big puffy coats will keep your friends warm. Bundle up so you can play too!

During the day, the sun slides across the sky, lighting up the world below. At sunset, colors fill the horizon, and the sun dips out of sight.

Can you guess what happens next?

ANSWER

As the sun sets, day turns into night. The sky goes dark. Several hours later, the sun rises to begin another day.

Sunflower plants sprout from the ground and grow. Then their flowers burst into bloom. If you look closely at a flower, you'll see its seeds.

If you plant a seed, what will happen next?

ANSWER

A new sunflower plant will sprout and grow. A plant's life cycle starts with a seed. Plants make seeds as their flowers bloom.

Animals are living. They breathe and grow and run and play. Plants are also living. They breathe and grow too. If a squirrel buries an acorn, an oak tree might sprout. If a squirrel buries a pebble, what happens?

ANSWER

Nothing. A pebble is not living, so it won't grow.

A baby sea turtle scrapes her flippers across the sand. She's newly hatched from an egg and trying to reach water. She'll live most of her life in the ocean, where she'll swim, eat, and mate. What will happen when she returns to the beach?

ANSWER

After mating, a female sea turtle crawls up on land to lay eggs, so more baby sea turtles can be born. Adults usually spend time on land only to lay eggs.

This monarch larva was born from a tiny egg. The caterpillar eats and grows. When it's big and full, it will spin a cocoon and crawl inside. What happens next?

ANSWER

Metamorphosis—that means the caterpillar will change inside the cocoon. When it pops out, it will be a monarch butterfly.

Some animals live in tough places. Special traits called "adaptations" help these animals survive. In the desert, food and water can be hard to find. Camels store fat in their humps. What happens when hungry camels can't find any food?

ANSWER

When food can't be found, camels break down the fat in their humps for extra energy. The humps get smaller as the camel uses up the fat.

Plants need water, just like people do. But a plant doesn't drink like you. When it rains, water falls to the ground. How does the plant get a drink?

ANSWER

The plant soaks up water with its roots. Roots also hold plants in the ground.

In fall, leaves turn color and drop from the trees. They litter the ground with red and yellow. Insects and worms then munch and chew up the leaves. What happens after the bugs and grubs have had their fill?

ANSWER

The insects and worms poop out waste to create compost. This mix of rotting leaves and waste is rich in nutrients. It helps more plants grow.

The sun beats down and the grass grows. A zebra grazes on grass to get energy to run. Then along comes a lion to pounce on the zebra. But what is big enough to hunt a lion for food?

ANSWER

Nothing. The cycle of a zebra eating grass and a lion eating the zebra is called a food chain. Lions are on top of the food chain, so nothing hunts them.

Ever hear of the dodo?
These large, flightless birds
lived in forests on an island in
the Indian Ocean. But people
cut down the forests.
What do you think happened
to the dodo bird then?

ANSWER

Dodos became extinct. They no longer exist in nature, because they don't have a place to live anymore. Can you think of other animals that became extinct?

What's that plastic bottle doing on the beach? Why is there an empty pop can lying in the grass? There have to be better uses for this trash. What could happen if you recycle that bottle and can?

Here's a hint: You can make things out of recycled materials.

ANSWER

27

You could have new playground equipment or a park bench to sit on. Recycling trash is one way to protect and respect nature.

How many of your predictions were correct? Did you know a lot about nature or learn something new? If you watch closely, you can begin to understand nature's wonders. You can make your own predictions and see if they come true.

GLOSSARY

compost—a mixture of decaying leaves, vegetables, and other items

extinct—no longer living; an extinct animal is one that has died out, with no more of its kind

horizon—the line where the sky and the earth seem to meet

larva—an insect at the stage of development between an egg and an adult

mate—to join together to produce young

metamorphosis—changing from one form into a very different form, like a caterpillar to a butterfly

nutrient—a part of food that is used for growth

predict—to guess what will happen in the future

recycle—to make used items into new products; people can recycle items such as rubber, glass, plastic, and aluminum

READ MORE

Burke, Lisa. *Backyard: Fun Experiments for Budding Scientists.* I'm a Scientist. New York: DK, 2010.

Thomas, Elizabeth. *Reduce, Reuse, Recycle.* Changing Habits, Living Green. Mankato, Minn.: Child's World, 2012.

Weber, Belinda. *I Wonder Why Caterpillars Eat So Much and Other Questions About Life Cycles.* I Wonder Why. Boston: Kingfisher, 2012.

INTERNET SITES

FactHound offers a safe, fun way to find Internet sites related to this book. All of the sites on FactHound have been researched by our staff.

Here's all you do:

Visit *www.facthound.com*

Type in this code: 9781429687218

Super-cool stuff!

Check out projects, games and lots more at
www.capstonekids.com

A+ books are published by Capstone Press,
1710 Roe Crest Drive, North Mankato, MN 56003
www.capstonepub.com

Library of Congress Cataloging-in-Publication Data
Hoena, B. A.
If you plant a seed– and other nature predictions / by Blake A. Hoena.
p. cm.—(A+ books. If books)
Includes bibliographical references.
Summary: "Simple text and full-color photos invite readers to make fun predictions
about nature"—Provided by publisher.
ISBN 978-1-4296-9251-9 (paperback)
ISBN 978-1-4296-8721-8 (library binding)
ISBN: 978-1-62065-194-0 (ebook PDF)
1. Nature study—Juvenile literature. 2. Nature observation—Juvenile literature. 3. Wildlife watching—Juvenile literature. I. Title.
QH48.H54 2012
508.072'3—dc23   2012008827

Credits

Jeni Wittrock, editor; Ted Williams, designer; Svetlana Zhurkin, media researcher; Laura Manthe,
    production specialist

Photo Credits

Alamy: Vova Pomortzeff, 26; Capstone Studio: Karon Dubke, cover, 3 (inset), 5, 9, 15 (all), 21, 28; Dreamstime: Chris Kruger,
23, Galyna Andrushko, 19, George Muresan, 6, Neilrod, 18; Getty Images: Photo Researchers,
25; iStockphoto: Goran Kapor, 16; Shutterstock: Alena Ozerova, 4, Ariel Bravy, 10, beltsazar, 13, Beth Van Trees, 29, Chris
Driscoll, 14, Hway Kiong Lim, 11, Iv Nikolny, 24, Jim Barber, 1, Kokhanchikov, 22, Login (question background), throughout,
Onur Ersin, 20, Pakhnyushcha, 3, Péter Gudella, 12, prism68, 27, Richard
Williamson, 8, Studio Barcelona, 9 (inset), tan4ikk, 7, Tracy Whiteside, 2, Vladimir Melnik, 17

Note to Parents, Teachers, and Librarians

This If Book uses full color photographs and fun text to introduce K–2 nature concepts in an interactive, predictive format. *If You
Plant a Seed . . . And Other Nature Predictions* is designed to be read aloud to a pre-reader or to be read independently by
an early reader. Photographs help listeners and early readers understand the text and concepts discussed. The book encourages
further learning by including the following sections: Glossary, Read More, and Internet Sites. Early readers may need assistance
using these features.

Printed in the United States of America in
North Mankato, Minnesota.
042012   006682CGF12